The Scramble for Africa: The History and Legacy of the Colonization of
Africa by European Nations during the New Imperialism Era

By Charles River Editors

The Rhodes Colossus Striding from Cape Town to Cairo, a cartoon that appeared in
Punch, December 10, 1892

About Charles River Editors

Charles River Editors provides superior editing and original writing services across the digital publishing industry, with the expertise to create digital content for publishers across a vast range of subject matter. In addition to providing original digital content for third party publishers, we also republish civilization's greatest literary works, bringing them to new generations of readers via ebooks.

Sign up here to receive updates about free books as we publish them, and visit Our Kindle Author Page to browse today's free promotions and our most recently published Kindle titles.

Introduction

Contemporary illustration of Major Marchand's trek across Africa in 1898

The Scramble for Africa

"The British South-African Company's shares
May be at a discount—(Trade-martyrs!—trade-martyrs!)—
But he, our Colossus, strides on, he declares,
Whether with or without chums or charters—or charters.
Hooray! We brave Britons are right now to the front—
Provided we've someone to boss us—to boss us;
And Scuttlers will have their work cut out to shunt

This stalwart, far-striding Colossus—Colossus!" – Excerpt from an editorial in *Punch*, December 10, 1892

The modern history of Africa was, until very recently, written on behalf of the indigenous races by the white man, who had forcefully entered the continent during a particularly hubristic and dynamic phase of European history. In 1884, Prince Otto von Bismark, the German chancellor, brought the plenipotentiaries of all major powers of Europe together, to deal with Africa's colonization in such a manner as to avoid provocation of war. This event—known as the Berlin Conference of 1884-1885—galvanized a phenomenon that came to be known as the Scramble for Africa. The conference established two fundamental rules for European seizure of Africa. The first of these was that no recognition of annexation would granted without evidence of a practical occupation, and the second, that a practical occupation would be deemed unlawful without a formal appeal for protection made on behalf of a territory by its leader, a plea that must be committed to paper in the form of a legal treaty.

This began a rush, spearheaded mainly by European commercial interests in the form of Chartered Companies, to penetrate the African interior and woo its leadership with guns, trinkets and alcohol, and having thus obtained their marks or seals upon spurious treaties, begin establishing boundaries of future European African colonies. The ease with which this was achieved was due to the fact that, at that point, traditional African leadership was disunited, and the people had just staggered back from centuries of concussion inflicted by the slave trade. Thus, to usurp authority, to intimidate an already broken society, and to play one leader against the other was a diplomatic task so childishly simple, the matter was wrapped up, for the most part, in less than a decade.

There were some exceptions to this, however, the most notable of which was perhaps the Zulu Nation, a centralized monarchy of enormous military prowess that required a British colonial war, the much storied Anglo-Zulu War of 1879, to affect pacification. Another was the amaNdebele, an offshoot of the Zulu, established as early as the 1830s in the southeastern quarter of what would become Rhodesia, and later still, Zimbabwe, in the future. Both were powerful, centralized monarchies, fortified by an organized and aggressive professional army, subdivided into regiments, and owing fanatical loyalty to the crown. The Zulu were not dealt with by treaty, and their history is perhaps the subject of another episode of this series, but the amaNdebele were, and early European treaty and concession gatherers were required to tread with great caution as they entered their lands. It would be a long time before the inevitable course of history forced the amaNdebele to submit to European domination. Although treaties and British gunboat diplomacy played a role, it was ultimately war, conquest, and defeat in battle that brought the amaNdebele to heel.

Despite this, the amaNdebele, notwithstanding their eventual military defeat, commanded enormous respect from the British. This was also true with the Zulu. The British were a martial nation themselves, and they saw the concept of the "Noble Savage" as the romance of a bygone age, offering up the esteem due to a ruling aristocracy, according to the rules of chivalry. With the defeat of the amaNdebele in 1893—in a war that has come to be known as the *Matabele*

War—agents of the British South Africa Company, as they assumed full administrative control of the territory, also established a rule of lionizing the amaNdebele. It became fashionable to mythologize the amaNdebele's noble origins, their courage and virtuosity in battle, and their incorruptible adherence to the Spartan code of war.

The Scramble for Africa: The History and Legacy of the Colonization of Africa by European Nations during the New Imperialism Era examines the turbulent history of imperialism across Africa and the consequences it has had. Along with pictures of important people, places, and events, you will learn about the Scramble for Africa like never before.

The Scramble for Africa: The History and Legacy of the Colonization of Africa by European Nations during the New Imperialism Era

About Charles River Editors

Introduction

Free Books by Charles River Editors

Discounted Books by Charles River Editors

The Berlin Conference

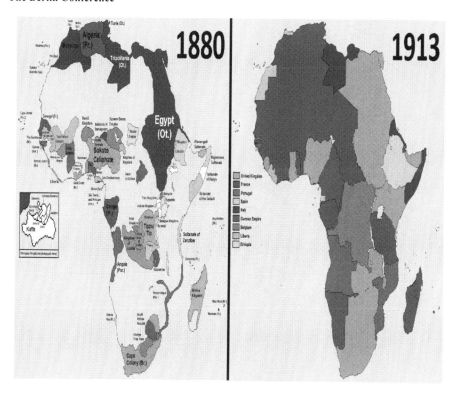

A map of African colonies in 1880 and 1913

"I do not want to miss a good chance of getting us a slice of this magnificent African cake." – Leopold II of Belgium

On the morning of Saturday, November 15, 1884, plenipotentiaries of all of the major powers of Europe gathered at the official residence of the German Reich Chancellor, Prince Otto von Bismarck. As each entered the yard, they were met at their carriage door by the Chancellor himself and then ushered into the library, where an informal reception took place. Then, as a body, they climbed the wide, ceremonial staircase to a second-floor reception room, where each took his allocated seat at a semi-circular table arranged before a large and detailed map of Africa pinned to the wall. Bismarck addressed the assembled delegates, outlining briefly the objectives of the meeting, after which, casting his eyes from left to right, he declared the Berlin Conference formally in session.

Bismarck

A depiction of Bismarck at the Berlin Conference

The Berlin Conference of 1884-85, a dry and rather formal affair, was nonetheless one of the most important and far-reaching gatherings of international power to take place at any time during the 19th century, and one that would deeply impact the course of European and African history up to the present day. In its simplest terms, the Berlin Conference sought to regulate the subdivision of Africa between the principal European powers in a manner that would not cause a major war between them. Only a somewhat desultory European interest had been shown in Africa to date, amounting to little more than a patchwork of competing spheres of influence. These were mostly private concerns — chartered companies displaying a national flag — but here and there, territories were being annexed and occupied, and in general, a rather unhealthy mood of competition was incubating over the question of Africa.

Perhaps the best example of this was the Witwatersrand, the gold-bearing region of the Transvaal Republic, nominally a British sphere of influence and certainly the most important theatre of British capital adventure of the age. South Africa at that point was divided into four separate territories - two British colonies (Natal and Cape) and two independent Boer republics (Transvaal and Orange Free State) - and between these there existed enormous suspicion and antipathy. The superior weight of British capital and imperial reach allowed the British to dominate the Transvaal gold fields, but they did so very much to the chagrin of the Boer. The Boer were not by any means impoverished because of this, but as they prospered, they were ever vigilant toward any British threat against their sovereignty.

It was onto this rather tense economic and political stage that the Germans entered in 1884, annexing the territory of Damaraland, nominally the whole of modern-day Namibia, as a German colony. This immediately pitched the British into a fit of apprehension. What were German intentions? Was it the gold, the diamonds, the strategic ports, or all of the above? The British were acutely aware that the hatred felt toward them by the Boer could easily drive them into the arms of an opposing European power, and bearing in mind the ideological compatibility of Germany and Boer at that time, the Germans were in a position, should they choose, to wreak havoc on British interests in South Africa.

Then, perhaps, the signature event took place that set the tone for some sort of orchestration of competing interests in Africa. In 1877, Welsh American explorer Henry Morton Stanley emerged at the mouth of the Congo River, completing an expedition of 1,000 days to map the central lakes complex and explore the Congo River. Here was the definitive, Victorian template of African exploration. Stanley, known by the natives of the interior as *Bula Matari*, or the Breaker of Rocks, had left Zanzibar in 1874, traveling over land toward the continental divide, where his objective was to map the lakes of the Great Rift Valley, determine the source of the Nile, and explore the Lualaba River.

Stanley

Three years earlier, in 1871, Stanley made his name as an explorer through his successful search for Dr. David Livingstone. Livingstone had not been heard from in Africa since departing England in 1866, also in search of the source of the Nile, and the general assumption was that he was dead. Stanley at that time was a roving reporter for the *New York Herald*, and sensing a scoop, publisher James Gordon Bennett commissioned and funded an expedition, led by Stanley, to search the African interior to either locate Livingstone or confirm his death. On November 10, 1871, Stanley achieved precisely this, finding Livingstone impoverished and ill in the settlement of Ujiji, on the east shore of Lake Tanganyika, and greeting him, at least according to popular myth, with the now immortal words "Doctor Livingstone, I presume."

Livingstone

Despite his lamentable circumstances, Livingstone would not contemplate leaving. His work, he maintained, was here in Africa. But he shared with Stanley his conviction that a large river he had discovered, flowing northward through what would today be northern Zambia and southern Congo, and known as the Lualaba, was the mythical source of the River Nile. Stanley disagreed, suggesting that it was more likely to be the headwater of the Congo River, and it was to confirm this, and much else besides, that Stanley embarked on his second expedition in 1874.

And with his emergence at the mouth of the Congo River in 1877, his hair now white, he confirmed his theory, and he was hailed in all the usual places as the greatest explorer of the age. Stanley, however, while hardly shunning the publicity, had in mind much more than just the fame of a great explorer. His journey down the Congo River had alerted him to the fact that here lay a region ripe for commercial exploitation. The Congo River, for all its mythical isolation, was in fact easily navigable for most of its length, and it offered therefore the opportunity to any stout-hearted nation to exploit an almost unimaginable wealth of gold and ivory, the staples of African trade that had made so many fortunes already.

With a flair for self-aggrandizement, Stanley began immediately to lecture and publish, beginning in England but wending his way through all the great capitals of Europe. His mission was simply to urge any and all who would listen to seize the opportunity to claim the Congo and win for themselves not only the prodigious economic prize on offer, but also a great moral opportunity to stamp out the last embers of the East African Slave Trade, then flourishing in anonymity in the dark heart of Africa.

A picture of slaves captured from the Congo on an Arab slave trader

At that point in history, however, the general European mood was conservative, and in Britain in particular, under the leadership of Prime Minister Benjamin Disraeli, there was a notable disinterest in assuming any additional fiscal responsibility in Africa. And although there was only standing room at every lecture and his books flew off the shelves, there was a conspicuous coolness all over Europe over the question of annexation.

In one very minor European capital, however, Stanley's exhortations were being taken very seriously. King Leopold II, titular monarch of Belgium, was taking very careful note, and through emissaries and intermediaries, he was subtly pursuing Stanley.

King Leopold II of Belgium

Leopold emerges from the pages of history as a curious character. He was a member of a privileged clique of European monarchs, bereft of power but rich, indulgent, and indolent. Leopold certainly availed himself of all the pleasures of court life, but he was also shrewd, astonishingly competent, and avaricious to an almost unimaginable degree. His initial interest in foreign real estate was imperial, insofar as he desired on behalf of Belgium the main accoutrements of a first-rate power, which were, of course, foreign estates and colonies. He was, however, unable to move the Belgian parliament to act in accordance, the conservative belief perhaps being that Belgium could not afford to compete on that level. Belgium was a small

European nation, existing between major and, at times, belligerent powers, and as such, it quietly went about its business with a determination not to rock the European boat.

Despairing of that avenue, Leopold next began to try and acquire a foreign colony on his own account. He sought at various times to buy a province of Argentina, to lease the Philippines from Spain, and to acquire from the French a quarter of Indo-China. None of these schemes amounted to much, but then, abruptly, in 1877, an upstart explorer by the name of Henry Morton Stanley emerged from the mouth of the Congo River, proclaiming to the world that here lay the next great El Dorado. This, Leopold realized, was his opportunity. He held his breath as Stanley toured the capitals of Europe, and as one by one they politely declined his importuning, he allowed his own interest to be known.

Once the fanfare of Stanley's celebrity had died down somewhat and realizing that he was unlikely to succeed where he most hoped, he settled for the second-class option and accepted an invitation to visit Leopold at the Royal Palace Laeken. Here he was lavishly feted and entertained, until, in due course, Leopold made him an offer. If Stanley would return to the Congo and begin establishing on Leopold's behalf the necessary infrastructure to conduct trade — those being a railway line around the first rapids and thereafter river stations and— this would establish Leopold's *prima petition* over the Congo, and for his efforts, Stanley would be amply rewarded.

To this, Stanley agreed, and in due course he set off back to the Congo. This left Leopold with the ticklish diplomatic conundrum of securing international recognition. Certain features of Stanley's account had caught his attention, and one was the rampant proliferation of slavery on the upper reaches of the Congo, originating from the slave markets of Zanzibar and supplying a thriving black market in slaves across the Arab world.[1] This, he decided, would be his *cause célèbre*. His opening move was simply to announce to the world his intention of forming an international organization to combat slavery in the Congo, which, in an age of abolition, was an extremely potent and shrewd maneuver. To satisfy the more mercantile interests of the ruling classes of Europe, he offered up the Congo River as an international free trade zone, and to capture the interests of the United States, he suggested the Congo as a destination to repatriate free-born blacks and freed slaves.

In combination, all of this represented an unstoppable momentum, and displaying enormous ability and a masterful grasp of diplomatic maneuver, Leopold was able to secure primary rights over the territory of the Congo River catchment, a portion of the globe more than three times the size of France. By any standards, this was a monumental coup, and by the time the other European powers woke up to precisely what was underway, it was too late the arrest the momentum.

---

[1] The East African Slave Trade had by then been outlawed, but it continued on the back of the ivory trade. Slaves were captured in the first instance by Swahili traders to portage ivory to the coast, and were sold thereafter as a secondary commodity.

Of all the issues on the agenda as delegates gathered in Berlin in 1884, foremost was the Congo question. The matter was debated, and although deeply troubled by the potential consequences, recognition was eventually afforded to Leopold's claim to the Congo. And so, the Congo Free State came into being, a private fiefdom of Leopold II of Belgium and arguably one of the most cynical and exploitative colonial regimes across the European spectrum. The truth of this would not immediately come to light, and the high-minded proclamations that accompanied the formation of Leopold's colony were taken at face value. However, it was of profound importance was to ensure that nothing like it could happen again, and central to the agenda of the conference, which lasted almost a year, was to establish certain ground rules governing the future European partition of Africa.

Of these, three are most noteworthy. The first was that the annexation of any territory in Africa by any European power would not be formally recognized without a clear display of effective occupation and administration. Second, no such annexation could proceed without a formal request for protection on the part of an indigenous leader or monarch responsible for that territory. Such a plea for protection would be required to be submitted to treaty and be ascribed with the seal, mark, or signature of that king. The third rule, which could perhaps be better described as a convention, required that in the event of a European war, the territories, protectorates, and colonies acquired under the terms of the conference's General Act would remain neutral.

The Source of the Nile

"Support a compatriot against a native, however the former may blunder or plunder." - Sir Richard Burton

In the spring of 1488, a small flotilla of Portuguese caravels rounded the southern peninsula of Africa, which they named the Cape of Storms, or the Cabo das Tormentas, making a brief landfall that marked a stupendous moment in global navigation. The sea lanes to the Far East now lay open, and soon afterward, it was the Portuguese again who would confirm this by making the first-recorded European maritime landfall in India. This achievement, however, was perhaps of greater impact to Africa than it was to India. En-route to India, the Portuguese seeded settlements, forts, and trade depots along the entire coast of sub-Saharan Africa, commencing the Atlantic Slave Trade and beginning an imperial relationship with Africa that would endure for the next 500 years.

Centuries before any other European power showed any interest in Africa, the Portuguese were active in trade and exploration. The two major Portuguese-speaking regions of Africa today are Mozambique and Angola, both founded during this period and both with some of the oldest European settlements anywhere south of the Sahara. The Portuguese, however, although a great maritime nation and voracious traders, proved ultimately to be a weak colonial power, and as the 19th century dawned and as other European powers began to show an interest in the continent, the Portuguese were slow to stake their claim over regions that they had roamed for centuries and long regarded as their own by virtue of prior claim.

Early European interest in Africa seldom progressed beyond the prosecution of the Slave Trade. The development of New World colonies, particularly the plantation colonies of Central and South America, the Caribbean, and the southern states of the United States, required labor, and Africa offered an unlimited resource. The kings and chiefs of the West African coast proved amenable to this arrangement, and thereafter, European penetration was limited to the coastal regions and the healthier climes to the extreme south. A combination of malaria and native resistance kept Europeans at bay, and this *modus vivendi* of trade endured in comfortable equilibrium until the dawn of the Age of Enlightenment.

Then came questions of humanity, of individual rights, and of the common brotherhood of man. From this arose the abolition movement, slow to start, but having gained momentum by the end of the 18th century, the institution of slavery had become so deeply discredited that its abolition was only a matter of time.

A matter of time, indeed, but also a matter of circumstance, the development of steam power and the evolution of anti-malarial prophylactics somewhat eased conditions for white labor in the tropics, and the acute dependence of colonial economies on slave labor from Africa gradually became less of a factor. The process, of course, was laborious, but in 1833, the British parliament passed a bill outlawing the trade in slaves throughout the British Empire, followed eight years later by an absolute ban. The British now claimed moral leadership of the civilized world, and soon the principal British interest in Africa shifted from the prosecution of the slave trade to its abolition. At about the same time and in combination, missionary activity in the immediate coastal hinterlands of Africa increased. The original spheres of influence established by the various European slave and general depots then tended to inform the denominations and languages of those missionaries, and thereafter the nationalities of the hunters and explorers who began to probe deeper into the interior. Here lay the basis of the division of territory, and before long, extensive stretches of the African coast began to organically subdivide according to European languages.

The interior, however, remained a blank map, and notwithstanding historic Portuguese involvement in many regions of the interior, formal exploration in the manner by which it would be recognized today only began with the first central European engagement, which was, in many respects, the starting pistol for the later partition known as the Scramble for Africa. The main geographic conundrums tended to be related to the rivers and the general drainage of the continent — the linking, for example, of known rivers, such as the Congo, the Niger, and the Nile, with their courses and their mouths.

The first explorers to achieve some measure of fame in this field were Mungo Park, a Scottish voyager who, between 1794 and 1803, mapped the course of the Niger River, and James Bruce, who in 1770 claimed the discovery of the source of the Blue Nile. Arguably the greatest African explorer — if not in terms of achievement, then certainly in fame — was Dr. David Livingstone, and the latter phases of his career were devoted to the discovery of the source of the Nile. This he never discovered, but the matter absorbed the British exploration community until Stanley, circumnavigating Lake Nyanza Victoria, confirmed English explorer John Hanning Speke's theory that the outflow of the lake at Jinja, on the north bank of Lake Victoria, represented the source of the Nile.

Park

Bruce

All of this was the stuff of *Boys' Own* adventure, and although the esoteric points of geography that defined this feature thrilled the Victorian public, they served a more practical purpose in filling in the blanks of the African map. By the 1880s, as Leopold was putting the finishing touches to his Congo coup, the main geographic features of the continent — the drainage systems of the central lakes region, the main mountains and watersheds, the deserts and the rivers — were all known and understood. It now began to dawn on the European capital element, most particularly the British, that Africa represented not only a vast resource of cheap raw materials, but also an almost unlimited potential market for European manufactured products.

The mantra of European expansionism in Africa now became *Christianity and Commerce*, the first of which was the preserve of the missionaries to introduce the standards of European, Christian civilization to the natives and the second, the preserve of the capital imperialists, which was to offer up an alternative avenue of wealth to the elites of Africa to simply capturing and selling one another. The process, of course, was rich with cynicism, and it was driven by the capital imperative of various European chartered companies with the backing and support of their governments.

Philanthropy Plus Five Percent

"Remember that you are an Englishman, and have consequently won first prize in the lottery of life." - Cecil John Rhodes

Soon after the publication of the General Act of the Berlin Conference, the Portuguese published what came to be known as the Pink Map, or the *Mapa cor-de-rosa*, which was the Portuguese response to the advent of the Berlin Conference. The Portuguese were the senior colonists of Africa, but as a maritime trading nation, they had over the centuries tended to confine themselves to their coastal ports, and so could not, under the terms of the General Act, display effective occupation and administration. Nonetheless, they felt a strong sense that their claim to much of the south-central interior of Africa was legitimate, and the Pink Map was an attempt to formalize this fact.

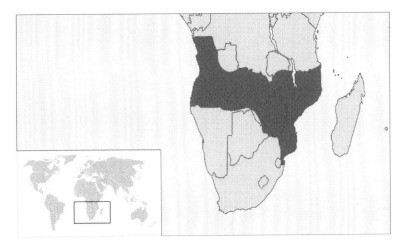

The Pink Map

The Portuguese pictured a unified belt, stretching from their west African territory of Angola to their east African colony of Mozambique and encompassing a swathe of territory including most of modern-day Malawi, Zambia, and Zimbabwe. At the same time, the Germans held substantive sway over two major territories in Africa, German East and German South West Africa, corresponding broadly with modern-day Namibia and Tanzania. They too pictured a belt of German territory linking these two major possessions, not dissimilar to the Pink Map, but larger and colored black.

As things stood in Europe at that time, the Germans probably had the more viable claim, because Portugal, notwithstanding its long legacy in Africa, was regarded as the poor man of Europe and not taken particularly seriously in this regard. The Portuguese manifestly lacked the resources to effectively enforce or back up such a claim, and in general the contest for this territory was between the Germans and the British. The French, it must be added, were no less active at this point in Africa, but their sphere of influence tended to be focused on West Africa, and we will touch on that little later.

The British, however, were now concentrated and very firmly established in the south. As already mentioned, the British held two major colonies in the southern sub-continent, the Cape and Natal, but the British were also extremely influential on the gold fields of the Transvaal, and they had much to lose by yielding to either Portuguese or German ambitions over the as yet unclaimed region of the interior, bearing in mind that this would immediately frustrate British advances north out of the southern sub-continent, which certainly defined the wider British objective in Africa.

That objective, however, was driven very much by one man — one of the most important personalities on the stage of British imperialism in Africa — a young British diamond magnate by the name of Cecil John Rhodes. Rhodes was a very curious character, and although very much a product of his age, he was also uniquely committed to the project of British territorial advancement in Africa. This was for many reasons, but essentially Rhodes was of a generation that believed with utter certainty that the English-speaking races enjoyed a God-given mandate to rule. "I contend," he was often heard to say, "that we are the finest race in the world and that the more of the world we inhabit, the better it is for the human race."

Rhodes

While a statement such as that will set modern teeth on edge and raise the hackles of egalitarians worldwide, it was nonetheless a commonly held view at the time. Since the destiny of the world lay in one way or another under European control, it was the opinion of Rhodes and many others like him that the fairest fate for any subject peoples would be to fall subject not to the German Empire, nor the French, and not the Portuguese, but to *Pax Britannica*. Rhodes defined the British view of imperialism as "Philanthropy plus Five Percent," implying by this that the principal objective of imperialism was to improve the world — Christianity and Commerce indeed — and moreover to do so in a profitable manner for all concerned. Of course, history would eventually confirm how this high-minded ideal went awry, but nonetheless, British imperialism was founded on that principal, and Rhodes, for all of his subsequent notoriety, believed in it as a simple article of faith.

Thus, what Cecil Rhodes pictured in ideal terms was the map of Africa painted not in pink, black, or blue, but in British red. Rhodes was based at the Cape, and in more practical terms, he settled for a rail and telegraph link between Cape Town and Cairo, linking British interests in

South Africa to British interests in North Africa by the acquisition and control of all of the territory in between. So quite clearly, Portuguese and German ambitions, particularly the latter, clashed in the most fundamental way with those of the British.

It's important to note that Cecil John Rhodes occupied no official government position, but was merely a businessman with vast imperial ambitions, and this tends to underline the fact that while the Scramble of Africa was a European imperial adventure, it was driven forward in many instances by private capital under the impetus of chartered companies. Rhodes was deeply frustrated by what he saw as a lack of British commitment in checking German ambitions in the region. He was driven to a ferment of anxiety by the German annexation of Damaraland, which he saw as an obvious move toward further German advancement north to link up with East Africa, which would effectively encircle British interests in South Africa and stunt any further British advance north. He succeeded in the end, through unremitting persistence, to persuade the British government to declare the territory of Bechuanaland, the future Botswana, a British protectorate, but the key to the ambitions of all three powers lay in control of Mashonaland.

Imperial Filibuster

"Until the lions have their own historians, the history of the hunt will always glorify the hunter." - Chinua Achebe

When looking at a modern map of Africa, one can very easily see the strategic importance, regarding these conflicting ambitions, of the central region today covered by southern Zambia, Malawi, and Zimbabwe. Here lay the key to advancement in all directions, and central to all of this was Mashonaland. Mashonaland is today the central province of Zimbabwe, but in the late 1880s, it was a vaguely understood region of the interior that held a far greater strategic than practical value, and it thus became central to a bout of power play that in many respects defined the very concept of the Scramble for Africa.

It's necessary to remember the central theme of the Berlin Conference: the rule that annexation must be proceeded by a plea for protection issued per treaty by whatever local leadership could be reasonably identified. Across the game board of Africa, insofar as the game had so far been played, this had been relatively easy. African leadership was, for the most part, fractured and divided, and for commercial treaty gatherers, trading guns, alcohol, and promises of armed alliance (to play one off against the other and thus gain control of vast regions of territory) was little less than child's play. In a handful of instances, however, this process was complicated by the existence of powerful, centralized monarchies who were not intimidated by threats or seduced by guns or alcohol, nor concerned about soliciting European support to crush some inconvenient neighbor. Here, frontier diplomacy could often prove very complicated indeed, and this was certainly true in the case of Mashonaland.

Here the tribes lay under the rule of a most storied military race, the amaNdebele, a blood and ideological relative of the Zulu race, under the control of a powerful monarch by the name of Lobengula. The chief *kraal* of Lobengula was kuBulawayo, the site of the modern-day Zimbabwean city of Bulawayo, its literal translation being "the Place of Slaughter."

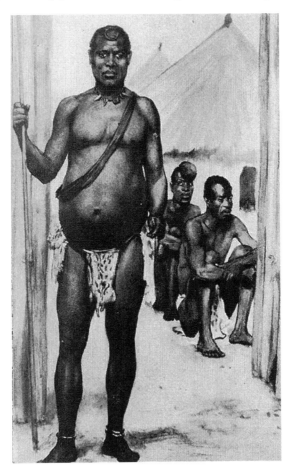

Lobengula

Lobengula's court, however, was under siege by an army of foreign treaty gatherers and concession seekers, representing private and public interests from across the entire European imperial spectrum. The king found himself in a dreadful quandary, for his military leadership (*indunas*) and his fighting regiments (*impis*) were urging him to order an advance on kuBulawayo to massacre these Europeans, which could have been achieved in less than an hour. Lobengula, however, was shrewd enough to know that his minor kingdom, as powerful as it was on a local landscape, could not match the power of those great empires whose representatives clamored with one another for his seal. He knew that an armed reaction at that moment, as tempting as it was, would simply invite a massive and crushing military response. On each of his borders, European powers were pressing, and it was a tide that could not be turned. For him to salvage something on behalf of his people, it would be necessary for him to yield to some degree to the pressure. The difficulty lay in determining to whom he would grant rights of access, for each one derided the other, and bearing in mind that he and all his advisors were illiterate, he had no idea who he could trust and who he could not.

Then, one day in October 1888, a small entourage appeared at the gates of his royal kraal, and three Englishmen requested an audience. This he refused, but they presented themselves before him anyway, and ignoring protocols that they approach on their knees, they introduced themselves as representing the British crown, through the agency of a certain powerful induna by the name of Cecil John Rhodes. The name was not entirely foreign to Lobengula, but he could not then have realized the impact that it would soon have on him and his people.

The manner in which these men, led by a tall and austere character by the name of Charles Dunell Rudd, had entered upon his court suggested the supreme confidence of a deputation supported by the immense power and reach of the British Empire. This, of course, was not entirely true, for Rhodes was acting in his private capacity, but if that was the impression, his ambassadors certainly made no effort to debunk it. Rhodes in fact enjoyed only a certain amount of official support from the British High Commissioner at the Cape, for example, and a great many other British officials on the ground in South Africa, but he lacked the formal endorsement of the crown, and so this was, indeed, strictly a private endeavor.

Rudd

Rhodes had decided that he would proceed by way of a chartered company. Chartered companies were no new idea. The British East India Company had forged the passage for eventual British rule in India, and, of course, the Hudson Bay Company had established the territorial precedent that would in due course become British Canada. More locally, the Royal Niger Company had established the basis of the future Nigeria, and the Royal East Africa Company did likewise for Kenya and Uganda, all under the same basic rules. Those rules were defined by a royal charter, issued by an imperial government and defining the rights and responsibilities of the grantee. A royal charter, in most cases, approved a wide prerogative for the company to occupy, annex, settle, pacify, govern, and exploit territories, usually as a precursor to formal, imperial rule. To a greater or lesser extent, all major powers engaged in African colonization did so through the expedient of chartered companies, with the rationale simply being to establish spheres of influence at private expense with the option at some later point of formal annexation.

It was vital, however, that Rhodes secure the all-important treaty with Lobengula before he could annex Mashonaland, and Rudd was under orders to achieve that end at all costs. Lobengula, meanwhile, arrived at the somewhat inevitable conclusion that his safest course of action was to deal with the strongest of his enemies, and in recognition of the fact that the British

Empire was the first among equals of Europeans powers, and in respect of the confidence shown by Rudd and the reputation of his superior, Lobengula decided, after lengthy and painful prevarication, to grant Cecil John Rhodes his coveted treaty.

Here, however, things get a little shady. Once the news that Rudd had stolen the prize from under their noses became general among the various concession seekers encamped outside kuBulawayo, Lobengula was inundated with intrigues and declaimers against Rhodes. However, one of the very few whites whom the king trusted was a Protestant missionary by the name of Charles Daniel Helm, one of a handful of missionaries granted access to the kingdom. Helm was fully conversant in isiNdebele, and he provided Lobengula with his personal guarantee that Rhodes could be trusted. Lobengula then stated several non-negotiable stipulations, the first of which was that all white men entering his kingdom under the terms of this treaty abide by his laws, and the second that no more than 10 individuals cross his borders at a time and for the limited purpose of prospecting for gold. To this, all parties agreed, and a concession document was drafted. The Reverend Helm confirmed to Lobengula that those terms stipulated were included in the written text, after which it was duly signed. Rudd immediately mounted a waiting horse and galloped off on the long road south to Kimberley, where he triumphantly handed the document to Rhodes, who in turn set off immediately for London to submit his application for a royal charter.

The truth of the matter, however, is that Charles Helm lied. The written text of the document contained none of Lobengula's principal clauses, granting instead a wide prerogative to the concession holder to enter and undertake mining and commercial activities in all Lobengula's territories. This was a de facto open invitation for colonization, and one can easily imagine that Rhodes's competitors were not slow to alert Lobengula to that fact.

It is tempting also to wonder why the Reverend Helm would have done such a thing, bearing in mind that he was among Lobengula's most trusted confidantes, and by all accounts, the two were authentic friends. To this, the answer lies in Helm's paramount loyalty to God and the British Empire. The amaNdebele were a military people, and they implanted a reign of terror on all surrounding people, and within the kingdom, the orthodoxy of life and loyalty to the crown was achieved by the exercise of a regime of profound brutality. If he could be instrumental in destroying this regime and replacing it with a system of British rule, British law, and British protection, the land would be a better place for it. Herein lies the essence of Christianity and Commerce, and if the sacrifice to achieve this was merely the outrage of a cruel and anachronistic monarch, then that was small price to pay.

Meanwhile, Lobengula issued an immediate recant on the document, thereafter known as the Rudd Concession, and demanded the return of the original. By then, of course, the original was in London, lying on the desk of the Colonial Secretary, Lord Knutsford, alongside an application for a royal charter, and the pleadings of a wronged, savage king in some faraway quarter of

Africa sounded very mute indeed. Lobengula then sent an embassy to London in the care of one of Rhodes's rivals. These two men, elderly induna both, were greeted by the press and public as a curiosity and paraded here and there as subjects of Her Majesty's empire. They were introduced to Queen Victoria, who received them with courtesy and responded to their pleas with polite platitudes. They were then dispatched on a tour of Royal Naval facilities in Portsmouth and then to the garrison town of Aldershot, where they observed a demonstration of machine gun and artillery fire. The two thereafter returned to kuBulawayo and reported to the king the utter futility of their situation.

A portrait of Lord Knutsford

If a defense of Cecil John Rhodes is possible, it would perhaps be that, like Helm, his belief simply was that, although the African people might at first squirm and resist, once the light of Anglo-Saxon civilization shone upon them, they would unfurl, bask, and proliferate. It is also true that Rhodes suffered from a heart disorder and asthma, and it was his belief, borne out by events, that he would not enjoy a long life. If even a small part of his vast vision would be achieved in his lifetime, he could afford no delays, and in every respect, time was of the essence.

Be that as it may, however, the saga of the Rudd Concession lingers in the popular memory of modern Zimbabwe as the first and greatest betrayal by the British of the African people. It nonetheless was sufficient to win Rhodes his royal charter, and in 1889, the British South Africa Company was incorporated. Rhodes thereafter began to plan the occupation and colonization of Mashonaland.

Anatomy of an Annexation

"[The Portuguese are] …an utterly effete worn out used up syphilitic race." – Dr. David Livingstone

Lobengula way well have been outmaneuvered, but he was still the master of a powerful military force, which, although it may not have stood for long against the might of the British Empire, could certainly deal with any attempt by a private corporation to invade his territory. This, therefore, was Rhodes's conundrum, and he adopted a strategy of calling Lobengula's bluff, insofar as Lobengula knew that the amaNdebele could easily wipe out a column of company pioneers, but that by doing so they would invite upon themselves eventual annihilation. A decade earlier, in 1879, the much more powerful Zulu nation had been relatively easily defeated in battle by the British and found themselves subject to British rule, and the same fate would await the amaNdebele if Lobengual did not play his cards very carefully.

The British South Africa Company Pioneer Column entered what was then known as Matabeleland from British Bechuanaland in July of 1890. It comprised a 200-man police force and some 190 civilian volunteers, and despite a great deal of threat and bluster, it was never attacked. On September 13, 1890, the Union Jack, that fabled flag of the British Empire, was raised upon a makeshift flagpole at the newly named Fort Salisbury, and to the sound of a 21-gun salute, the British colony of Rhodesia was born.

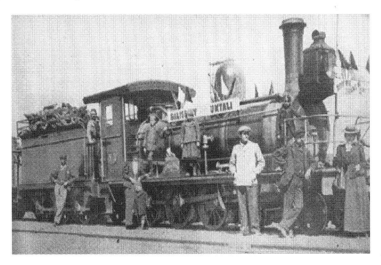

A picture of the railway opening in Rhodesia

The amaNdebele were indeed eventually broken in battle, their classic, set-piece formations cut down by the concentrated musketry and machine gun fire of a much smaller British South Africa Company force. Three years later, the nation rose in rebellion once more and was again defeated. This added the territory of Matabeleland as a province of the future Rhodesia, a colony named after its founder, Cecil John Rhodes.

Meanwhile, having secured Mashonaland, and effectively frustrating German and Portuguese efforts to do the same, Rhodes now moved quickly to expand that advantage. British South Africa Company agents quickly crossed the Zambezi River and began the process of acquiring treaties and concessions among tribal chiefs and headmen, preparing the groundwork for Rhodes' seizure on behalf of the British crown of all the unclaimed territories up to the southern borders of Leopold's Congo.

Having occupied his new colony, Rhodes was immediately confronted by the practical reality of sustaining a landlocked holding deep in the interior, via a long, overland supply line from the Cape. Eastward there lay the Portuguese territory of East Africa, the future Mozambique. Without a clearly defined frontier, however, and certainly without effective occupation or administration, the territory was, practically speaking, there for the taking. And if Company forces could lay effective claim to the hinterland of Portuguese East Africa, then there would seem to be no reason why they should not press on to the Indian Ocean, lay claim to a portion of the Mozambique seaboard, and acquire for the new territory a port.

Thus, almost before the news of the successful occupation had reached the British press, British South Africa Company agents were en route east to search out the principal chiefs and headmen to acquire the necessary treaties. The Portuguese, however, were alerted to this, and dispatched to the same area a much larger force of Angolan levies under Portuguese command, and what followed was an ugly cut and thrust along an ill-defined frontier. This saw the forces of the British South Africa Company roundly humiliate a much large Portuguese force, a Portuguese colonel clapped in irons and shipped back to Cape Town, and a British journalist killed and eaten by a lion.

The way, however, was clear to the coast, and in one of the great epics of the age, a handful of men set off across the fever-ridden coastal plain of East Africa to seize the port of Beira. It was an act of naked international piracy, and from the Cape, Rhodes urged his men on, assuring them that no matter what happened, if they marched into Beira and presented Her Majesty with a *fait accompli*, he would square the matter up afterward.

The British High Commissioner at the Cape, Sir Henry Loch, no friend of Cecil Rhodes, caught wind of what was afoot and sent a British military officer by express sail to the Port of Beira, and the incoming British South Africa Police detachment was intercepted and warned in the strongest terms possible to cease and desist. The Portuguese government complained bitterly to the British government, and Rhodes was severely censured. Nonetheless, the territorial advantage went to the British South Africa Company, and the final boundary settlement between the two countries fixed the frontier along the escarpment of the central plateau, gaining the Company some 100 miles of territory at the expense of the Portuguese.

SIR H. B. LOCH,
Chief Commissioner at the Cape.

Loch

Meanwhile, further to the north, where Rhodes's agents were scouring the country for the usual treaties of protection, another of the great personalities of the Scramble for Africa stepped onto the stage. Sir Harry Johnston, arguably the quintessential British imperialist, matched wits with the Germans and the Portuguese to secure the boundaries of what would, in due course, become the British territories of Nyasaland (Malawi) and Northern Rhodesia (Zambia).

Johnston

The Little Prancing Proconsul

"[W]hy should we have bothered to negotiate with Negroes, Arabs, Afghans, Siamese, Malays, or Papuans?" - Sir Harry Johnston

The European colonization of Africa, in almost every instance, was preceded by the arrival of missionaries, and these usually set the tone for the slow influx of Europeans that would follow; no better example of this is there than the protectorate of Nyasaland. Lake Nyasa, the future Lake Malawi, was discovered, if such is an appropriate term, by Dr. Livingstone, who was himself a missionary and an avid anti-slavery campaigner. He also happened to be Scottish. It was thanks to this that the first missionary establishments founded in the region of Lake Nyasa, the future Malawi, tended also to be Scottish.

It was likewise under Scottish management that the first commercial enterprise was established on the lake. The African Lakes Company, founded in 1877, in the absence of any formal administration, provided the only non-native government in the region. This pitched the

Portuguese, again affixed to the east coast, into a fit of apprehension, for once again, this was a region of the interior that they had long regarded as falling within their sphere of influence. Another factor that rendered this particular province of the interior so significant is that it was populous and thus popular with both Arab and Portuguese slave traders, plying a trade that had by then been internationally outlawed.

The presence of British personnel, in the form of missionaries and traders, placed a responsibility on the shoulders of the British government to establish some sort of an official presence in any particular region, and this it did first by the appointment of British consuls. This was the case for Nyasaland, but these men where limited in authority and certainly in capacity, and all that can perhaps be said of them was that they uniformly echoed one another in calling on the British government to establish a more robust presence in the region, first and foremost to stamp out the slave trade. The attitude of the British Imperial government, however, was ambivalent. So long as the Portuguese were making no aggressive attempts to enforce their claim, there seemed no reason to commit resources to its defense, and although the eradication of slavery was the responsibility of all signatories to the Main Act of the Berlin Conference, this was often accompanied by a conspicuous official lethargy. The Portuguese were beleaguered on many fronts, and on the eve of the Berlin Conference, they offered no threat to anyone outside of the immediate administrative zone of a handful of coastal ports and settlements.

The Portuguese were not and never really had been the problem. The British, as ever, were watching what the Germans were up to with more interest than in the Portuguese. An agent of the German East Africa Company, a short, compact, and deceptively bookish-looking character by the name of Carl Peters, was touring the territories adjacent to the island of Zanzibar, engaged in the usual activity of securing treaties of protection from various chiefs and tribal leaders. What, the British wondered, were German intentions regarding the unclaimed hinterland, the same territory Cecil John Rhodes was hankering for with his own minor army of treaty and concession seekers?

Throughout much of this region, Arabs and Arabized Africans existed, as they had done for centuries, as the main force of trade, a trade headquartered and controlled from the Island of Zanzibar. The nominal domains of the Sultan of Zanzibar covered almost the entirety of this region and were utilized by agents of the sultan and other Islamic elements of Swahili/Arabic origin as the main trade catchment for the trade in slaves and ivory. To confront them, no force existed other than a handful of dominant tribes who were themselves heavily implicated in the slave trade. With the findings of the Berlin Conference published and with a growing interest on the part of the various European powers now difficult to ignore, the Arabs and Swahili began to arm themselves and stood ready to defend their historic trade interests. It was a tense region, but again, it was there for the taking.

Into this picture stepped Sir Harry Hamilton Johnston, the British proconsul, marking the point at which the three-way balance of power in the lake region began to shift in the direction of the British. At some point during 1888, and confirmed by Rhodes's shenanigans on the border of Portuguese East Africa, the British Government had finally arrived at a decision regarding the nature and extent of British interest in Africa. While British Prime Minister Lord Salisbury shared none of Rhodes's grand delusions of a crimson swathe from the Cape to Cairo, he did find himself of the opinion that what mattered most was south and east Africa. A free hand was to be given to the French in the west in the hope that their interest would be diverted from Egypt, while the Portuguese, a force hardly to be reckoned with, would have to live with the reality that the Pink Map was dead.

Harry Johnston, or Sir Harry, is one of the enduring characters of the British colonial period, an imperialist to the marrow of his bones, an artist, writer, philosopher, explorer, naturalist, and archeologist; the list is almost endless. In the spring of 1889, he was appointed proconsul for the lakes region of Nyasaland, prior to which employment he was appointed chief negotiator to the Portuguese government, charged with negotiating the future boundary between British and Portuguese spheres of influence, which in practical terms simply meant breaking it to them that their grand ambitions in Africa were being subordinated to the British.

That very spring, however, Cecil John Rhodes was in London, lobbying the British parliament to grant his royal charter, and the two men happened to meet, and experiencing an instantaneous meeting of minds, the single biggest obstacle to a British political initiative in Nyasaland, finance, was overcome. In exchange, Johnston agreed to act on Rhodes' behalf to secure the necessary treaties to British South Africa Company control of all territories between the Zambezi River, including the mineral-rich Katanga, then under the control of Leopold's Congo, although he acknowledged that this might be stretching the rules just a little too far. Soon afterward, Johnston set sail for Lisbon, and soon after that he embarked for Mozambique, en route to Nyasaland.

Upon arrival, he found himself confronted by hostile overtures on two fronts. The Portuguese, in a maneuver that Johnston rightly recognized as saving face, had dispatched an armed force up the Zambezi River and in the direction of Lake Nyasa, intending, ostensibly, to plant the Portuguese flag on what they maintained was Portuguese soil. Secondly, a war had broken out on the north of the lake between the African Lakes Company and a powerful local cartel of Swahili/Arab slave traders, led by a particularly powerful and ruthless warlord by the name of Mlozi.

The dynamics of the East African Slave Trade differed in many key aspects to the more storied Atlantic Slave Trade. The East African trade was ancient and bound up in the traditions of Islam and Sharia Law. Its markets were concentrated in the Arabian Peninsula and the Persian Gulf, and it lay in the hands of familial branches of the Sultanate of Oman and the Sultanate of

Zanzibar. The entire trade had been outlawed under international treaty in 1873, but it continued to thrive throughout east and central Africa as an illegal trade, eventually overlapping the continental divide and spilling into the expanses of the Congo Basin. It was this, incidentally, that formed the basis of Leopold's philanthropic sham in establishing the Congo Free State.

As increased European interest in these regions shone an unwelcomed light on the activities of organized slave traders, so those traders grew more militant and aggressive, seeking fresh fields to ply their trade. It is perhaps worth noting that the enforcement of abolition in the western hemisphere drove many rogue Portuguese slave traders around the Cape to the less heavily policed waters of the Indian Ocean, which in turn caused an acceleration of the trade in areas controlled by the Portuguese, underwriting much of their activities up the Zambezi Valley. It is also true that the development of the French plantation islands of the Indian Ocean added to the demand, all of which pitched the incoming colonial regimes, such as that beginning to take root in Nyasaland against the remnants of this dying institution, the death throes of which were both violent and desperate.

Standing in the way of the advance of slave traders southward into the lakes region was nothing more than the missionaries, who were unarmed, and the sole white factor of the African Lakes Company, a certain stalwart Scotsman by the name of L. Monteith Fotheringham, supported by an inventory of eight loyal "station boys", 13 old *Chassepôt* rifles, and 34 damp cartridges. Sir Harry Johnston carried the mandate of the crown, and as such it was his duty to act on behalf of that crown in attending to any instances of war against the slave traders.

Dealing with the Portuguese proved in the end to be relatively easy. On his journey upriver toward Nyasaland, Johnston encountered the Portuguese force, comprising some 1,200 native levies under the command of Portuguese Colonel Alexandre de Serpa Pinto. Over tea and biscuits one afternoon, served in bone china on a linen-draped table and under the ample shade of a baobab tree, the matter was discussed. Sir Harry, fluent in Portuguese and sipping his tea with his little finger erect, pondered aloud the wisdom of Portugal provoking a war with Britain over a minor piece of African real estate. The matter had, after all, been broached in Lisbon between he himself and Prime Minister José Luciano de Castro (Sir Harry was then, as always, willing to drop names), and that any local breaches of that diplomatic protocol could hardly serve the career of an ambitious young army colonel.

Colonel de Serpa Pinto

As Colonel de Serpa Pinto then hurried back downriver to consult with his superiors, Sir Harry continued upstream to deal with the Arabs. The war, such as it was, was in a stalemate, and initially, with no force of his own to call upon, Sir Harry negotiated a ceasefire and temporary truce between the Arabs and the company men, allowing both for the time being to live and let live. This would stand for a while, since both sides were exhausted and both Mlozi and the African Lakes Company were teetering on the brink of bankruptcy.

Johnston now had to consider his obligations to Cecil John Rhodes, and again, a glance at a map of southern Africa provides a sense of the geopolitical jigsaw puzzle that was beginning to fall into place. Southern Rhodesia, broadly defined as modern-day Zimbabwe, was now an established British territory, bordering Portuguese East Africa to the east and British Bechuanaland in the west. To the south lay South Africa, its fate awaiting the outcome of the

Anglo/Boer War, a decade into the future, and to the north the unclaimed territories of the future Northern Rhodesia. Nyasaland, a long sliver of territory bordering Lake Nyasa, was now reasonably well established as a British territory, and all that remained was to mark that point on the map that the Germans, now entrenched on the coast of Tanganyika, with the southwestern boundary of their interests and the northeastern boundary of British interests, had as yet not defined.

Lakes, rivers, and mountain ranges, as always, provided obvious lines of demarcation, but in this case, an avenue existed between the northern tip of Lake Nyasa and the southern tip of Lake Tanganyika through which German treaty gatherers might easily penetrate and begin to mop up territory vital to the interests of the British. It was to this region, therefore, that Sir Harry next made his way.

And in typical style, with his sketchpad and notebook in hand, Johnston made a record of the botany, the landscapes, and languages, as well as the peculiarities of race and appearance, culture, religion, fetish, and morality, which in due course contributed to his astonishingly detailed description of Nyasaland, entitled *British Central Africa*, and later his *A Comparative Study of Bantu and Semi-Bantu Languages*. He sojourned briefly with the missionaries of the London Missionary Society station on the southern tip of Lake Tanganyika, gathering copious treaties from local chiefs, observing as he did, "One feels at this distance of time that to readers of a new generation this treaty-making in Africa must seem a farce. Great European States would meet at conferences to partition Africa, Asia, Papuasia, Melanesia into spheres of influence between themselves: why should we have bothered to negotiate with Negroes, Arabs, Afghans, Siamese, Malays, or Papuans?"

Despite their illiteracy, Johnston went on to note that native chiefs and councilmen submitted to memory the terms of any agreement made, placed excellent value on the terms agreed to, and in the main were faithful to those terms. Most treaties were simply standardized documents, which in effect did little more than indicate that peace existed between a certain tribe and the Queen of England. The local leader, whatever rank he might have held and whatever authority he may have commanded, was bound over to alienate no territory or sovereignty to any other European power without Her Majesty's approval and was furthermore obliged to freely admit British citizens and to accord Her Majesty consular jurisdiction over all disputes that might arise between the indigenous inhabitants and those citizens. Despite what might be said or offered in negotiations for the various signatures that held these treaties legal, no specific protection was given, promised, or offered.

Having thereby secured the northern boundaries of Northern Rhodesia, Johnston was poised to sail up Lake Tanganyika in the London Missionary Society sailboat to gather treaties in the Rwanda region in the interests of Rhodes's Cape to Cairo vision, but he was brought back to reality abruptly by news that the Portuguese had resumed their aggressive approaches and were now situated in force at the southern end of Lake Nyasa, meaning that war between Portugal and Britain was once again imminent.

Johnston hurried south, taking the opportunity to declare the territory a British protectorate. The date of this was September 25, 1889, after which any further Portuguese movement in the direction of British Nyasaland would amount to a declaration of war. Two months later, however, Colonel Serpa Pinto did indeed make that move, ordering an armed advance into Nyasaland, news of which reached London in mid-December. Sensing his opportunity, British Prime Minister Lord Salisbury responded quickly, and against a patriotic drum-roll from the British public, he issued the Portuguese an ultimatum, reinforced by the deployment of the Channel Fleet to the mouth of the Tagus with sealed orders and the dispatch of a Royal Navy squadron from Zanzibar to Mozambique. In the face of such a virile response, Portugal had no choice but to climb down.

This, combined with Rhodes's shenanigans over the seizure of the port of Beira and the ultimate loss to Portugal of both territory and prestige, was an experience deeply scarring, which, although relatively quickly forgotten in Britain, was neither forgotten nor forgiven in Portugal. The government fell, the windows of the British consulate were stoned, and members of the British expatriate community in the northern city of Oporto were insulted and jostled in the streets. Black crepe was draped over the statue of Luís de Camões, the poet whose masterpiece *Os Lusíadas* celebrated Portugal's golden period of the 15th and 16th centuries. Although many months would elapse before a final settlement of the matter was submitted to treaty, to Portugal this was the end of a long-cherished dream and the first real indication that she was not to be numbered among the principal power brokers in the new world order.

Meanwhile, Sir Harry's administration was, in 1893, reinforced by a strong detachment of Sikh soldiers on loan from the Indian Army, then a British colonial force, and these, along with their officers, were deployed to finally bring an end to the persistent trade in slaves along the shores of Lake Nyasa, taking the opportunity at the same time to impress upon any independent-minded tribes that the region now lay under British control.

The final denouement with the slavers came with a last and conclusive action against the stockade of the Swahili/Arab slave trader Mlozi. A long siege followed that resulted in Mlozi's eventual surrender, his prompt trial, and hanging, and thus, with that salutary action, the last incidence of organized slavery in any British territory in Africa was brought to an end.

On the Wider Stage

"I cannot make it better known than it already is that I strongly favor colonization." – Abraham Lincoln

While all of this went on, there was a wider field of activity. In the end, the only European nation to acquire a territorial assemblage in Africa comparable to the British were the French, and although the French played no part in southern Africa, unless the French Indian Ocean islands can be regarded as southern Africa, they were a major player in West Africa and North Africa.

Leopold's maneuvers in the Congo were the spark that set in motion the rush to claim and colonize Africa, but it was the French that attempted first to practically check his ambitions by the advance of their own practical claims to the Congo Basin. As Henry Morton Stanley worked on Leopold's behalf on the south bank of the Congo River, the French sought on the north bank to stake out a similar sphere of influence. The man at the forefront of this enterprise was another of those European imperial heroes, part poet and part imperialist, part idealist and part brigand.

Pierre Savorgnan de Brazza was the antithesis of Stanley. He was tall, handsome, ascetic, and socially conscious. His explorations in central Africa tended to be focused in the regions of modern-day Gabon and Congo Brazzaville, on the north bank of the Great Congo River, but once the practical ramifications of Leopold's scheming became clear, it was he who urged most forcefully a French intervention along the north bank to block the potential for Leopold extending his influence. This resulted in the establishment of the colony of French Congo, to which, in 1883, he was appointed governor. His regime of governorship was perhaps most notable for its leniency in an age of exploitation, and for this, ironically, he was removed in 1897.

Brazza

Brazza certainly was the exception rather than the rule in this regard, and it was his planting of the French flag in the equatorial region that led to the founding of the French territorial bloc later named French Equatorial Africa. This comprised four territories, today recognizable as Congo Brazzaville, Gabon, Central African Republic, and Chad. French West African interests, however, comprising a vast swathe of that region, began with very early French settlements in the territory of Senegal.

The modern nation state of Senegal occupies a point at the westernmost extremity of Africa, and it was ideally situated to serve as a strategic staging point for early Portuguese mariners as they began to probe down the west coast of Africa during the 15th century. The mouth of the

Senegal River marks one of the earliest points of European landfall, and for centuries it remained a staging point for rest and resupply before the journey south into the less hospitable expanses of Gulf of Guinea. Later, in the 17th century, the region fell under substantive French control and briefly under British control. The first permanent settlement was the Port of Saint-Louis, at the mouth of the Senegal River. This, in due course, became the most developed and most climatically suitable French settlement in the region, and therefore the platform from which much of the onward march of French territorial expansion in west and central Africa took place.

French sub-Saharan Africa eventually expanded to include two vast federated blocks, these being French Equatorial Africa, mentioned already and formally established in 1910, and French West Africa, established earlier in 1895 and comprising the territories of Senegal, Guinea, Côte d'Ivoire, French Sudan (later Mali), Mauritania, Niger, Upper Volta (later Burkina Faso), and Benin. Each was governed from Paris through two Governors General, one based in Dakar and another in Brazzaville, with deputies, or Lieutenants Governor, located in each territorial capital.

The French, of course, were extremely influential in North Africa too, and notwithstanding Napoleon's foray into Egypt, which was not an episode of the Scramble for Africa, the French laid claim to most of the southern Mediterranean, principally Algeria, which was treated as a province of France, as well as protectorates over the territories of Tunisia and French Morocco. Algeria would prove a bitter thorn in the French side as the Age of Imperialism matured, and so entrenched did the French become there that a war of peculiar ferocity was fought between 1954 and 1962 to defend French sovereignty against a liberation movement. It was this war that set in motion French decolonization and which brought down the French Fourth Republic.

In the west African region, however, the Germans acquired only two nominal territories: German Kamerun, now Cameroon, and German Togoland, now comprising Togo and parts of eastern Ghana.

The British, of course, were a major player here, as elsewhere, with the principal British west African territories being Nigeria, Ghana, Sierra Leone, and the Gambia. Of these, perhaps the only episode worth expanding on would be that of Sierra Leone, which was founded as a coastal settlement soon after the turn of the 19th century as a location to repatriate slaves freed on the high seas or in any other way liberated from slavery. It was only after the Berlin Conference and with each European power looking over its shoulder at the other that the British saw sense in establishing sovereignty over the interior of what would now be recognized as the modern nation of Sierra Leone.

Egypt existed under nominal and varying degrees of British protection from 1822 until 1956. It can be argued that this was not a chapter of African history but European history, since it was Egypt's strategic position in the Mediterranean, in particular regarding the Suez Canal, that made it of such enduring interest. The British maintained the fiction that their engagement was informal and diplomatic, but even though direct British rule was always questionable, the British held a firm grasp over the territory through two world wars, and arguably, if it had fallen to the Axis powers on either occasion, the outcomes might have been very different.

The Spanish waded into the whole business of African partition with a handful of colonial acquisitions on the mainland, namely Spanish North Africa, a partial annexation of Morocco, a legacy of which is the modern territorial enclave of Ceuta. Further south, the Spanish claimed Spanish West Africa, which was nominally attached to Morocco and which transitioned then from Spanish Sahara to what is now Western Sahara, a disputed independent territory on the West African coast. In the Gulf of Guinea, the Spanish held Spanish Guinea, now Equatorial Guinea, along with its associated islands. The Spanish, however, were never major players, and somewhat like the Portuguese, they were overshadowed by the French and the British and to a degree by the Germans.

Aside from Mozambique and Angola, the Portuguese held several smaller territories, based on historic claims that could not be disputed. If Portugal had been able to robustly defend these historic claims, then arguably she would have laid claim to the lion's share of West Africa, but as it transpired, all that remained were the islands of Cape Verde, São Tomé and Príncipe, Portuguese Guinea (now Guinea Bissau), and a handful of minor and short-lived enclaves.

Even the Russians entered the race, albeit very briefly, by annexing the Bay of Sagallou in modern day Djibouti in 1889. The reasons for this are vague, but the adventure survived one day short of a month and was never repeated.

It is debatable whether Italian engagement in Africa pertained to this era of colonization or to a later era better associated with the rise of fascism, for the only African territory that the Italians acquired during the era of European imperialism was Eritrea, and it was only nominally held. It was only later, under Benito Mussolini, that Italian possession expanded in the Horn of Africa to include Ethiopia and Somalia. The Italian conquest of coastal Libya took place in 1911, and it was also established as a unified colony under Mussolini in 1934.

Only two territories in Africa were not colonized in the formal sense of the word, and these were Ethiopia (which was occupied briefly by the Italians during World War II) and Liberia. The former, Ethiopia, existed during this period, as it had for centuries, as an imperial monarchy, and although various European powers held strong diplomatic interests in the country, it never became subject to formal annexation. Liberia, on the other hand, was a curiosity. It comprises a stretch of the West African coast that was known historically as the Pepper Coast, or the Grain Coast, as others were known as the Slave and Gold Coasts. It experienced periods of visitation by both the Portuguese and the British, but its permanent settlement by outsiders came about under very unusual circumstances.

At about the turn of the 19th century, a movement gathered momentum in the United States to repatriate free-born and freed blacks to Africa, in part to protect them from discrimination in the form of political disenfranchisement and the denial of civil, religious, and social privileges, and in part to remove them from the Southern states. In 1816, the American Colonization Society was founded for this purpose, and although not universally popular among blacks, repatriation, as it was termed, began in 1822. By 1867, the American Colonization Society and various state chapters had assisted in the migration of more than 13,000 blacks to Liberia.

The anomaly, however, revealed itself as these incoming colonists married within their own community and came eventually to identify themselves as Americo-Liberians, developing a specific ethnic identity with a cultural tradition infused with American ideals of political republicanism and Protestant Christianity. They did not identify with the indigenous peoples of the colony, especially those of the more isolated communities of the hinterland, who were regarded as primitive and backward.

As the colony matured, the Americo-Liberians established conservative and exclusive political mores and became in almost every respect a colonizing force with perhaps a more focused animosity against the indigenous people than white colonists in neighboring territories. In due course, the same frustrations and pressures began to build against them as they did against white colonists. The Liberian coup of 1980 was a particularly violent and brutal affair, as the ruling elite were replaced by an indigenous military junta, and thereafter, as history has borne out, Liberia became the venue for one of the most anarchic periods of civil war in modern African history.

Leopold's Congo, meanwhile, proved itself to be the virtual poster child of colonial horror and exploitation. Leopold had moved with alacrity to seal up the Congo the moment he was granted formal recognition, but the terms of free trade that had been offered did not materialize, and instead, private concessions were granted to exploit the resources of the Congo by whatever means were most effective. Violence and coercion on a scale never before and never since experienced were inflicted on the people of the Congo, and ivory and rubber were extracted at an almost incalculable cost in life and liberty.

Leopold escaped overt censure or criticism until a movement began to take shape in Britain to publicize and end the abuses under way. In 1908, the matter was taken up by the British parliament, and in due course pressure was brought to bear on the Belgian parliament to annex the territory and remove it from Leopold's private control. This was done in 1909, but before Leopold could be brought to account, he died in December of that year. How much revenue was accrued through these actions will always be speculative, but the figure was astronomical, and ironically, Leopold never at any time set foot in the colony.

With that, the geopolitical map of Africa, established during the Scramble for Africa, was solidified during the years preceding World War I, after which its final adjustments were made. The events of the Great War set in motion the end of global empire. It was fought on a truly global scale, and notwithstanding commitments made during the Berlin Conference, several major campaigns were fought on African soil. The Germans in general did not defend their colonies vigorously, believing that victory would be achieved in Europe, after which the Germans would reclaim not only their own, but all other European assets in Africa too.

Of course, that did not happen. The German, Russian, and Ottoman empires crumbled, and through the newly formed League of Nations, many of the individual territories once controlled by those empires were granted as mandates to the victorious powers. The British, therefore, inherited the German colony of Tanganyika, South Africa acquired South West Africa, and both the British and French assumed the colonies of Togoland and Cameroon. The Belgians retained the Congo and held on to it until 1960, when independence was granted.

World War II ultimately marked the end of European empire, and after Indian independence in 1947, the dominoes fell relatively quickly. The last substantive colonial territories to be granted independence were Rhodesia in 1980, Namibia in 1990, and South Africa in 1994.

Online Resources

Other books about African history by Charles River Editors

Other books about the Scramble for Africa on Amazon

Further Reading

Aldrich, Robert. Greater France: A History of French Overseas Expansion (1996)

Atkinson, David. "Constructing Italian Africa: Geography and Geopolitics." Italian colonialism (2005): 15–26.

Axelson, Eric. Portugal and the Scramble for Africa: 1875–1891 (Johannesburg, Witwatersrand UP, 1967)

Boddy-Evans, Alistair. "What Caused the Scramble for Africa?" African History (2012). online

Brantlinger, Patrick. "Victorians and Africans: The genealogy of the myth of the dark continent." Critical Inquiry (1985): 166–203. online

Chamberlain, Muriel Evelyn. The scramble for Africa (4th ed. Routledge, 2014) excerpt and text search

Curtin, Philip D. Disease and empire: The health of European Troops in the Conquest of Africa (Cambridge University Press, 1998)

Darwin, John. "Imperialism and the Victorians: The dynamics of territorial expansion." English Historical Review (1997) 112#447 pp: 614–642.

Finaldi, Giuseppe. Italian National Identity in the Scramble for Africa: Italy's African Wars in the Era of Nation-building, 1870–1900 (Peter Lang, 2009)

Gjerso, Jonas Fossli (2015). "The Scramble for East Africa: British Motives Reconsidered, 1884-95". Journal of Imperial and Commonwealth History. Taylor & Francis. 43 (5): 831–60. doi:10.1080/03086534.2015.1026131. Retrieved 4 March 2016.

Hammond, Richard James. Portugal and Africa, 1815–1910: a study in uneconomic imperialism (Stanford University Press, 1966)

Henderson, W. O. The German Colonial Empire, 1884–1919 (London: Frank Cass, 1993)

Hochschild, Adam (2006) [1998]. King Leopold's Ghost: A Story of Greed, Terror, and Heroism in Colonial Africa. London: Pan Books. ISBN 978-0-330-44198-8.

Klein, Martin A. Slavery and colonial rule in French West Africa (Cambridge University Press, 1998)

Lovejoy, Paul E. Transformations in slavery: a history of slavery in Africa (Cambridge University Press, 2011)

Lloyd, Trevor Owen. Empire: the history of the British Empire (2001).

Mackenzie J. M. The Partition of Africa, 1880–1900, and European Imperialism in the Nineteenth Century (London 1983).

Oliver, Roland, Sir Harry Johnston and the Scramble for Africa (1959) online

Pakenham, Thomas (1992) [1991]. The Scramble for Africa. London: Abacus. ISBN 978-0-349-10449-2.

Penrose E. F., ed. European Imperialism and the Partition of Africa (London 1975).

Perraudin, Michael, and Jürgen Zimmerer, eds. German colonialism and national identity (London: Taylor & Francis, 2010)

Robinson R,. and J. Gallagher, "The partition of Africa", in The New Cambridge Modern History vol XI, pp 593–640 (Cambridge, 1962).

Rotberg, Robert I. The Founder: Cecil Rhodes and the Pursuit of Power (1988) excerpt and text search; online

Sanderson G. N., "The European partition of Africa: Coincidence or conjuncture?" Journal of Imperial and Commonwealth History (1974) 3#1 pp 1–54.

Sparrow-Niang, J., Bath and the Nile Explorers: In commemoration of the 150th anniversary of Burton and Speke's encounter in Bath, September 1864, and their 'Nile Duel' which never happened(Bath: Bath Royal Literary & Scientific Institution, 2014)

Stoecker, Helmut. German imperialism in Africa: From the beginnings until the Second World War (Hurst & Co., 1986.)

Thomas, Antony. Rhodes: The Race for Africa (1997) excerpt and text search

Thompson, Virginia, and Richard Adloff. French West Africa (Stanford University Press, 1958)

Wesseling, H.L. and Arnold J. Pomerans. Divide and rule: The partition of Africa, 1880–1914 (Praeger, 1996.)

Free Books by Charles River Editors

We have brand new titles available for free most days of the week. To see which of our titles are currently free, click on this link.

Discounted Books by Charles River Editors

We have titles at a discount price of just 99 cents everyday. To see which of our titles are currently 99 cents, click on this link.

Made in the USA
Columbia, SC
05 June 2021

39081923R00028